Napo

Enjoy all our books for free…

 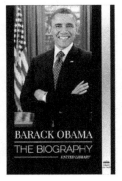 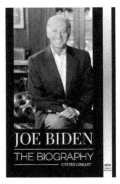

Interesting biographies, engaging introductions, and more.
Join the exclusive United Library reviewers club!
You will get a new book delivered in your inbox every Friday.

Join us today, go to: https://campsite.bio/unitedlibrary

Introduction

Napoleon Bonaparte was a French military general, the first emperor of France and one of the world's greatest military leaders.

Napoleon revolutionized military organization and training, sponsored the Napoleonic Code, reorganized education and established the long-lived Concordat with the papacy.

"Courage isn't having the strength to go on - it is going on when you don't have strength." - Napoleon Bonaparte

This is the descriptive and concise biography of Napoleon Bonaparte.

Table of Contents

Introduction 2
Table of Contents 3
Napoleon Bonarparte 5
Biography 10
   Youth 10
   Emperor of the French (1804-1815) 17
   Last years 37
Health status 41
Return of his ashes to France 43
Napoleonic Heritage 44
   Restoration of slavery 50
Achievements of Napoleon Bonaparte 54
   Under the Consulate 54
   Under the Empire 56
   Legislative work 57
   In architecture and urban planning 58
Titles and honours 61
   Title 61
   Foreign Decorations 62
Contemporary Perspectives 64
Nicknames 65
Privacy Policy 68
   Historical influences 68

Napoleon and Women 69
Napoleon and spirituality 70
Correspondence 75
Family 76
Marriages and children... 77
Order of succession to the imperial throne in July 1815.. 80
Preservation of the personal archives of Bonaparte and his family 81

Napoleon Bonarparte

Napoleon Bonaparte, born on 15 August 1769 in Ajaccio and died on 5 May 1821 on the island of St. Helena, was a French soldier and statesman, the first emperor of the French, from 18 May 1804 to 6 April 1814 and from 20 March to 22 June 1815, under the name **Napoleon I**.

Second child of Charles Bonaparte and Letizia Ramolino, Napoleon Bonaparte became a general in 1793 in the armies of the First French Republic, born of the Revolution, where he was commander-in-chief of the Italian army and then of the army of the East. He came to power in 1799 with the coup d'état of 18 Brumaire, and was First Consul - consul for life from 2 August 1802 - until 18 May 1804, when the Empire was proclaimed by a senatus-consulte followed by a plebiscite. He was crowned Emperor in the Cathedral of Notre-Dame de

Paris on December 2, 1804, by Pope Pius VII. His wife, Empress Josephine de Beauharnais, was also crowned.

As General-in-Chief and Head of State, Napoleon attempted to break up the coalitions set up and financed by the kingdom of Great Britain and which, from 1792 onwards, brought together the European monarchies against France and its regime born of the Revolution. He led the French armies from Italy to the Nile and from Austria to Prussia and Poland: Bonaparte's many brilliant victories (Arcole, Rivoli, Pyramids, Marengo, Austerlitz, Jena, Friedland), in rapid military campaigns, disbanded the first four coalitions. The successive peace, which put an end to each of these coalitions, strengthened France and gave Napoleon a degree of power that had rarely been equalled in Europe until the Peace of Tilsit (1807).

Napoleon lastingly reformed the State, restoring its authority and primacy. France underwent major reforms, making Napoleon one of the founding fathers of contemporary French institutions. In this sense, the Napoleonic codifications, including the 1804 Civil Code, made it possible to strengthen individual liberties or the equality of citizens before the law, by achieving a synthesis by guaranteeing certain revolutionary achievements and taking up traditional principles from the Ancien Régime. The French administration was reorganized, with the creation of prefects in the departments.

Similarly, a new currency emerges, the franc, while the Banque de France is established. The Conseil d'État was also created, as were the lycées. Napoleon also tried to reinforce the French colonial regime of the Ancien

Régime overseas, particularly with the re-establishment of slavery in 1802, which led to the war of Santo Domingo (1802-1803) and the definitive loss of the colony.

Napoleon brought the French territory to its maximum extension with 134 departments in 1812, transforming Rome, Hamburg, Barcelona or Amsterdam into the capitals of French departments. He was also President of the Italian Republic from 1802 to 1805, then King of Italy from 1805 to 1814, and also Mediator of the Swiss Confederation from 1803 to 1813 and Protector of the Confederation of the Rhine from 1806 to 1813. His victories allowed him to annex vast territories to France and to govern most of continental Europe by placing the members of his family on the thrones of several kingdoms: Joseph on that of Naples then of Spain, Louis on that of Holland, Jerome on that of Westphalia and his brother-in-law Joachim Murat in Naples. He also creates a duchy of Warsaw, without daring to formally restore Polish independence, and temporarily submits to his influence defeated powers such as the kingdom of Prussia and the empire of Austria.

Object of both a golden and a black legend during his lifetime, he owes his very great notoriety to his military skill, rewarded by numerous victories, and to his astonishing political trajectory, but also to his despotic and very centralized regime and his ambition, which resulted in very deadly wars of aggression (in Portugal, Spain and Russia) with hundreds of thousands of dead and wounded, military and civil, for the whole of Europe. He is considered one of the greatest commanders in history, and his wars and campaigns are studied in military schools around the world.

While he financed increasingly general coalitions, the Allies eventually achieved decisive successes in Spain (Battle of Vitoria) and Germany (Battle of Leipzig) in 1813. Napoleon's intransigence in the face of these setbacks caused him to lose the support of whole sections of the French nation, while his former allies or vassals turned against him.

He was forced to abdicate in 1814 after the capture of Paris, capital of the French Empire, and to withdraw to the island of Elba. He tried to regain power in France during the Hundred Days episode in 1815. Able to reconquer France and to re-establish the imperial regime there without a blow, he nevertheless brought the country to an impasse with the heavy defeat at Waterloo, which put an end to the Napoleonic Empire and ensured the restoration of the Bourbon dynasty. His death in exile, in St. Helena, under the custody of the English, is the subject of much controversy.

A romantic tradition makes Napoleon the archetype of the "great man" called to turn the world upside down. This is how the Count of Las Cases, author of the *St. Helena Memorial,* tried to present Napoleon to the British Parliament in a petition written in 1818.

Élie Faure, in his work *Napoleon,* which inspired Abel Gance, compares him to a "prophet of modern times". Other authors, such as Victor Hugo, called the defeated Saint Helena the "modern Prometheus". The shadow of "Napoleon the Great" hovers over many works by Balzac, Stendhal, Musset, but also by Dostoyevsky, Tolstoy and many others. In addition, a French political current emerged in the 19th century, Bonapartism, claiming to be the result of Napoleon's actions and mode of government.

"Take time to deliberate, but when the time for action comes, stop thinking and go in." - Napoleon Bonaparte

Biography

Youth

Birth

Napoleon Bonaparte was born in Ajaccio on August 15, 1769, day of the Holy Mary (patron saint of Corsica), in the family house, today transformed into museum. Napoleon was born one year after the treaty of Versailles, by which the republic of Genoa cedes Corsica to France; the island is thus recently French. He was baptized Napoleone Buonaparte (first name given in memory of an uncle who died in Corte in 1767), and was not baptized in the cathedral of Notre-Dame-de-l'Assomption in Ajaccio until July 21, 1771. The Bonaparte family is of Italian origin and came to Corsica at the end of the 15th century.Jean Tulard writes that, since 1616, the Bonaparte family have been members of the council of the Elders of Ajaccio; they are essentially notaries, lawyers, and are allied with former island seigniorial families

Napoleon was the fourth child (the second of the surviving children, after Joseph) of Charles Bonaparte, a lawyer on the island's High Council and court clerk, and Maria Letizia Ramolino, whose marriage had been celebrated in 1764.

Later, Napoleon made his birth date, August 15, a holiday: Saint-Napoleon's Day.

- the Legislature (or the "Dumb Body") passes or rejects laws ;

- the Conservative Senate is responsible for verifying that the law is consistent with the constitution.

The preparation of the law is the responsibility of the executive, through the Council of State, which is responsible for drafting legislation. Power functions in an authoritarian manner; the processes of semi-direct (somewhat fictitious) democracy are carefully organized and controlled. The consul himself corrects the results if they are not satisfactory.

Napoleon's speech to the Army after Italian Campaign Victories

On May 1796, Napoleon gave a speech to congratule the soldiers involved in the Italian campaign after a considerate number of victories in the battlefield.

The following is the speech:

"Soldiers: You have in fifteen days you have won six victories, taken twenty-one stand of colors, fifty-five pieces of cannon, and several fortresses, and overrun the richest part of Piedmont; you have made 15,000 prisoners, and killed or wounded upwards of 10,000 men. Hitherto you have been fighting for barren rocks, made memorable by your valor, though useless to your country, but your exploits now equal those of the armies of Holland and the Rhine. You were utterly destitute, and you have supplied all your wants. You have gained battles without cannon, passed rivers without bridges, performed forced marches without shoes, and bivouacked without strong liquors, and often without bread. None but Republican phalanxes, the soldiers of liberty, could have endured what you have done; thanks to you, soldiers, for your perseverance!

Your grateful country owes its safety to you; and if the taking of Toulon was an earnest of the immortal campaign of 1794, your present victories foretell one more glorious. The two armies which lately attacked you in full confidence, now fly before you in consternation; the perverse men who laughed at your distress, and inwardly rejoiced at the triumph of your enemies, are now confounded and trembling. But, soldiers, you have yet done nothing, for their still remains much to do. Neither Turin nor Milan are yours; the ashes of the conquerors of Tarquin are still trodden underfoot by the assassins of

Basseville.* It is said that there are some among you whose courage is shaken, and who would prefer returning to the summits of the Alps and Apennines. No, I cannot believe it. The victors of Montenotte, Millesimo, Dego, and Mondovi are eager to extend the glory of the French name!"

From consul to emperor

In 1800, Bonaparte attacked and defeated the Archduchy of Austria once again. Beaten at Marengo by Napoleon and at Hohenlinden by Moreau, the Austrians had to sign the Treaty of Lunéville on February 9, 1801, which led the British to sign the Peace of Amiens on March 25, 1802 (4 germinal year X, countersigned two days later). Although his power was fragile in the aftermath of Brumaire, Marengo's victory and its aftermath strongly consolidated Bonaparte's situation.

On December 24, 1800, while the Consul and his family were on their way to the opera house, they fell victim to an "infernal machine" (bomb) waiting for them on rue Saint-Nicaise. The First Consul's coachman gallops past. The bomb explodes too late and only the windows of the vehicle are blown out. On the spot, on the other hand, there is carnage. Twenty-two people were killed and about a hundred wounded. Fouché, then Minister of Police, succeeded in proving that the attack was the work of the royalists, led by a certain François-Joseph Carbon, while Bonaparte was convinced that he was dealing with the Jacobins.

In 1802, it is the peace of Amiens, the occasion for Napoleon to settle an old score with the journalist Jean-

Gabriel Peltier, exiled for 10 years in London and whose articles indisposed him. The King of England let it go, the trial opened on February 21, 1803 at Westminster. Although defended by James Mackintosh, J-G. Peltier is condemned, but the sentence will never be applied. More important and soon more serious, Bonaparte set in motion his grand design for America. Taking advantage of the now free movement of the French fleet in the Atlantic, he wanted to develop Louisiana, the immense territory on the right bank of the Mississippi River that had belonged to France since the secret signing of the Treaty of San Ildefonso in 1800.

To do so, it needs a secure base of operations. The colony of Santo Domingo is the perfect choice. From this bridgehead of France in the New World, it will be able to regain a foothold in New Orleans without rushing the young American state, which would see its westward expansion definitively circumscribed to the Mississippi.

But in Santo Domingo, Toussaint Louverture is an obstacle to this plan. The black general has been governor general of the colony on behalf of France since 1797 and is suspected of connivance with the United States with whom, in defiance of the principle of the Exclusive, he has traded openly since prosperity returned.

Moreover, the previous year he had the great planters, his objective allies, vote for an autonomist constitution proclaiming him governor general for life and had the audacity to send him to France for simple ratification, once the fact was accomplished. This act of open rebellion by a warlord reputed to be invincible and firmly attached to his island was timely to justify the size of the forces committed to the expedition that was being prepared. And the cold and imperious reason of state also justifies the re-establishment of slavery in the colonies of the New World, being argued that the great French Louisiana will have to develop quickly to gain speed with the English and Americans, which it could not do without the servile labor force that has proven itself so well in Santo Domingo.

This is why two fleets are sailing to the West Indies, Leclerc, Bonaparte's own brother-in-law, to Santo Domingo with 20,000 men and Richepanse to Guadeloupe with 3,400 men. These chiefs are provided with very explicit secret instructions written in Bonaparte's own hand. They were to take military control of the two colonies and disarm the indigenous officers before re-establishing slavery. Proclamations are ready, in French and Creole, to reassure the indigenous populations of Bonaparte's personal attachment to freedom. This plethora of precautions demonstrates that he understood that success or failure would depend on secrecy, and the facts proved him right.

After three months of fierce resistance, the old Toussaint Louverture, betrayed by his general officers skillfully undertaken by Leclerc, laid down his arms. Captured and deported to France, he died a few months later at Fort de Joux near Pontarlier. Leclerc could move on to the second phase of the plan and disarm the colored officers, but Richepance in Guadeloupe re-established slavery without delay and the news of this betrayal of the First Consul's word tipped Santo Domingo into insurrection. The expeditionary force, weakened by an epidemic of yellow fever, recedes everywhere. Leclerc obtained nearly

20,000 men for reinforcements, but the disease killed a third of the Europeans who reached these shores.

The General-in-Chief himself died on November 2, 1802. With his back to the sea, the remnants of his army will soon be forced to surrender by the soldiers of General Dessalines, who will proclaim the independence of the former colony under its former Indian name of Haiti.

The time of French America has already passed. At the beginning of 1803, the peace with England wavered and the Atlantic Ocean once again became a hostile sea. Declaring forfeiture, on April 30, Bonaparte paid Louisiana to the United States for eighty million francs.

After Bonaparte extended his influence over Switzerland (which returned to a decentralized organization after the unitary attempt of the brief Helvetic Republic (1798-1803)) and Germany, a dispute over Malta served as a pretext for the British to declare war on France again in 1803, and to support the royalist opposition to Bonaparte.

Royalist agents, including Charles Pichegru, clandestinely landed in France and contacted Georges Cadoudal and Jean Victor Moreau. The conspiracy is quickly revealed and its members arrested. Pichegru dies strangled in his cell; the others are tried and convicted. Cadoudal is executed, Moreau banished. But the conspiracy also makes a collateral victim: the Duke of Enghien, prince of blood. The First Consul has him abducted in foreign territory, summarily tried by a military commission and executed, following statements collected from Cadoudal after his arrest. The execution that takes place at Vincennes does not provoke any protests other than those of the United Kingdom, Russia and Austria.

Napoleon crowned himself emperor on December 2, 1804. Strictly speaking, the Empire was born at the request of the Senate. The historian Steven Englund agrees with the opinion that it was initially a question of "protecting" the Republic. When the Consulate was shot down, the *order* would have collapsed with it. The Empire, for its part, was an institution that sealed the durability of republican values. Napoleon Bonaparte could die: the heredity of the title was supposed to protect the country from upheavals and the loss of revolutionary gains. This is how the imperial coins bore the words "Napoleon Emperor - French Republic" until 1808.

In addition, a wise observer of the establishment of the Consulate and the Empire, the Countess of Remusat, explains how "men tired of revolutionary troubles" saw in Bonaparte the one who would "save them from the dangers of tumultuous anarchy" and bring them "rest under the domination of a skillful master, whom fortune seemed determined to assist".

"Ability is nothing without opportunity." - Napoleon Bonaparte

Emperor of the French (1804-1815)

Imperial Symbols

The imperial coronation, a unique event in the history of France, represented in Jacques-Louis David's painting

The Rite of Napoleon, is heavily laden with symbols. The passage from the Republic to the Empire required the creation of imperial coats of arms, as well as the creation of symbolic objects intended to establish a previously non-existent tradition. Napoleon, who wanted to bring people together, decided to associate to the symbols of his reign the images that may have previously represented France, as well as the strong European powers.

The eagle is chosen in reference to the Roman eagles, carried by the legions, but it is also the symbol of Charlemagne, the unfurled eagle. The red color of the imperial mantle is a direct reference to the purple of the Roman imperium. Napoleon thus poses as the heir of the Roman Empire and Charlemagne.

The bees are supposed to recall the Merovingians (brooches representing them having been found in tombs of that time), and their arrangement on the coat of arms and the imperial mantle must recall the fleurs-de-lis of the Capetians. The hand of justice, used by the Capetians during royal coronations, must show that the Emperor is the heir to their power. Napoleon wants to show that he is the founder of the "fourth dynasty", that of the Bonapartes, after the Merovingians, the Carolingians, and the Capetians.

Other symbols used during the sacrament are charged with moral values. Thus Napoleon holds for a moment the globe of Charlemagne; he wears the crown of this same emperor (these two elements having been forged from scratch before the coronation). His sword and scepter are said to be "Charlemagne's": they have actually been used for several centuries by the Valois and then the Bourbons during their coronations.

The Pope, present at the ceremony, is here only to bless his reign.

Napoleon and the Church

The signature of the Concordat by the First Consul in 1801 recognized Catholicism as the religion of "the majority of the French", and no longer as the state religion. Priests now received treatment from the state. In order to show his power, Napoleon will not be crowned in Rome, as Charlemagne and the Germanic emperors did in the past (until the 15th century); it is Pope Pius VII who will be brought to Paris. Napoleon welcomed him in the forest of Fontainebleau, on horseback and in hunting clothes, wanting to make people believe in the fortuitous nature of the meeting.

The rapprochement between Napoleon and the Church was the result of a political calculation on the part of the Emperor. Beyond the moral value of a religious coronation in the eyes of Catholics, the symbolic value of a pontifical coronation reminiscent of the coronation of Germanic emperors, Napoleon placed himself on an equal footing, even above the European kings as successor to Charlemagne and the emperors of ancient Rome. The Pope's presence at the coronation gives an additional moral and legitimate dimension to the Empire. It is no longer simply the fruit of a revolution, it is a divine coronation like that of other European sovereigns, but which none of them can equal.

Napoleon placed himself at the same level as the sovereign of the Holy Roman Empire before overtaking him to become the only emperor in Europe. François II had moreover understood it well since after the proclamation of the French Empire, he decreed that Austria, then archduchy, also became an empire.

The Pope's presence is therefore more a message to European countries than a profession of Catholic faith on the part of Napoleon. Napoleon, who was not very sensitive to the fate of the Pope, later held him prisoner in Fontainebleau. With the idea of asserting France's power in the spiritual realm, he even considered transferring the Pope's residence from Rome to Paris, before abandoning this idea. At the end of his life, Napoleon received extreme unction from the hands of Abbot Jean-François de Kermagnan.

Napoleon and the economy

Napoleon implemented numerous reforms in the societal and economic fields. He is at the origin of the construction of the Paris Stock Exchange and its main regulations.

In particular, he instituted the Civil Code, also known as the "Code Napoleon", promulgated on March 21, 1804 (30 Ventôse year XII), which takes up part of the articles of the Custom of Paris and the written law of the South of France, protecting the law of obligations and contracts. It also pushes for the development of cotton factories, installed in the national property, while the wars created a need for textiles to dress the armies. It is the industry he wishes to encourage the most. Close to Gabriel-Julien Ouvrard, a prestigious trader and munitions dealer, who operates import licenses in Nantes, his industrial projects suffered the consequences of the continental blockade, a Napoleonic decree that claimed to prohibit the European continent to any ship that had touched an English port.

While Portugal, a neutral country, allowed Brazilian cotton to be obtained through French traders, the emigration to Brazil of the Portuguese royal family in 1807, to flee the 30,000-strong French army commanded by Jean-Andoche Junot, who was marching on Portugal, triggered retaliatory measures against France, which was deprived of Brazilian cotton.

Napoleon also supported the art industries. In 1804, he recreated the Garde-Meuble, the institution responsible for furnishing the imperial palaces, and, through it, he had Parisian carpenters and cabinetmakers working. He was particularly attentive to them during the crises of 1807 and 1810-1811.

The Victorious Empire

In 1804, the time was not yet ripe for vast conquests, and, convinced for a long time that the only way to obtain a definitive peace was to neutralize the United Kingdom, Napoleon developed, with Admiral Latouche-Tréville (who died before he could execute it), a plan for the invasion of the United Kingdom. This ambition sank definitively at the battle of Trafalgar, where the Franco-Spanish fleet commanded by Admiral de Villeneuve was destroyed by that of Admiral Nelson. The United Kingdom gained domination of the seas for the next century.

In 1805, the Third Coalition was formed in Europe against Napoleon. The Emperor, who in Boulogne was overseeing preparations for the invasion of the United Kingdom, had to face a sudden war. He led an immediate offensive, taking the Grande Armée to Austria on a forced march, and secured a brilliant victory over Austria and Russia on December 2, 1805 at the Battle of Austerlitz, known as the "Battle of the Three Emperors".

In 1806, Prussia provoked a new conflict. The campaign that Napoleon leads ("the Spirit on the march", according to Hegel) is impressive of speed: he sweeps away the Prussian army at the battle of Jena (doubled by Davout's victory at Auerstaedt where, with 30,000 men, Marshal Davout defeats the 63,500 Prussians who attack him).

The following year, Napoleon crossed Poland, won a victory over the Russians in Friedland and finally signed, in Tilsit, in the middle of the Neman, in an interview staged to strike a chord, a treaty with Tsar Alexander I that divided Europe between the two powers.

Yet trained in the schools and by the masters of the Ancien Régime, as an officer in the royal army, Napoleon broke with the old military concepts. It was no longer a question of fighting a siege war with the help of 30,000 to 50,000 men, but of seeking the decisive battle, engaging more than 100,000 men if necessary. His objective is not to remain master of the battlefield, but to *annihilate* the enemy.

In 1808, Napoleon created the nobility of the Empire: soon his marshals and generals would bear the titles of Count of the Empire, Prince of Neuchâtel, Duke of Auerstaedt, Duke of Montebello, Duke of Danzig, Duke of Elchingen, King of Naples.

From September 27 to October 14, 1808, Napoleon met Alexander I in Erfurt for a new treaty, so that they could unite against the Austrian Empire, which threatened to redeclare war on France. The tsar refuses, preferring that this treaty be drawn up with the aim of renewing the alliance that had been forged between them the previous year in Tilsit; this in fact allows Napoleon to ensure Alexander's loyalty for even longer. But it is a failure because the emperor soon realizes the betrayal of Talleyrand, who had approached the tsar advising him to resist Napoleon, even if he was seduced.

"Strategy is the art of making use of time and space. I am less concerned about the latter than the former. Space we can recover, lost time never." - Napoleon Bonaparte

Campaigns in the Iberian Peninsula and Austria

Spanish War

In response to the British attitude towards French merchant ships, Napoleon attempted to impose the continental blockade, which aimed to asphyxiate British industry and trade, by the Berlin decree of 21 November 1806. Portugal, an old ally of the British since the Treaty of Methuen (1703), had remained neutral since the breaking of the peace of Amiens. Through diplomatic pressure, a closer alliance with neighboring Spain, and the concentration of troops on the Pyrenees in the summer of 1807, Napoleon threatened Portugal with invasion if he did not apply the continental blockade.

Faced with Portuguese silence, the French armies invaded Portugal (November 1807), commanded by General Junot, and also settled in Spain, as an ally, to provide support for this operation under the Treaty of Fontainebleau. The Portuguese court and government took refuge in Rio de Janeiro with the support of the British fleet and Brazil became the seat of the kingdom until 1821.

From the autumn of 1807, tensions increased at the head of the kingdom of Spain: King Charles IV threatened his son and heir Ferdinand, who was opposed to the stranglehold of the head of government, Manuel Godoy, on the royal couple and on Spanish politics. Napoleon then considers Spain, a disappointing ally in the war against Great Britain, as ripe for a dynastic change. This prospect panicked the Spanish monarchy and Godoy.

In March 1808, the Aranjuez uprising put Ferdinand on the throne, following the forced abdication of his father. Napoleon then positioned himself as arbiter of the Bourbon family of Spain, and took advantage of their quarrel to impose their complete abdication in Bayonne. Napoleon places on the Spanish throne his brother Joseph, replaced in Naples by Joachim Murat, husband of Caroline Bonaparte. The Spanish population rises: the Spanish War begins and will last six years. The British army commanded by the future Duke of Wellington landed in Portugal and the French suffered serious setbacks (surrender of Baylen in Spain, Battle of Vimeiro in Portugal) during the summer of 1808. With the help of Spanish patriots, the Anglo-Portuguese gradually pushed the French army out of the Iberian Peninsula.

Napoleon later admitted that he had made a serious mistake in launching the Spanish campaign: "This unfortunate war has lost me; all the circumstances of my disasters are connected to this fatal knot. It has complicated my embarrassment, divided my forces, destroyed my morality in Europe. Similarly, concerning Joseph, incapable of being head of state and of maintaining order: "He was the most incapable man and precisely the opposite of what was needed.

War against Austria

While the best troops of the French army are engaged in Spain, the Empire of Austria once again attacks France in Germany and Italy. Marshal Lannes, Napoleon's companion and friend, perishes at the Battle of Essling, which appears to be Napoleon's first great setback, as his troops must abandon the battlefield to take refuge on the island of Lobau, on the Danube, to rest and strengthen themselves. The Austrian army was finally defeated at the battle of Wagram in July 1809.

The year 1809 increased the imperial regime's sense of vulnerability: Napoleon was first wounded - slightly in the foot - at the Battle of Regensburg in April 1809, recalling his vulnerability as commander-in-chief in a battle, and then escaped an assassination attempt by

Frédéric Staps during a review of the troops at Schönbrunn on 12 October 1809, at the time of the conclusion of peace with the Austrian Empire. The vulnerability of the French sovereign reinforced the principle of ensuring a direct heir to the Empire.

Josephine's divorce was then inevitable, all the more so as Napoleon knew that the sterility of the couple was not of his doing, since the birth of little Léon, the fruit of an affair in 1806, and the very recent pregnancy of Marie Walewska, another affair initiated during the Polish campaign in 1807, who came to Vienna during the peace negotiations (the child, Alexandre Walewski, was born in May 1810).

Napoleon, sovereign of the "Great Empire".

A few months after the peace of Schönbrunn, on 2 April 1810, Napoleon married Archduchess Marie-Louise of Austria, the eldest daughter of his last enemy. On March 20, 1811, she gave him a son, after a long and painful childbirth, and this child was baptized "Napoleon François Charles Joseph" and given the title of *King of Rome*.

At the beginning of 1812, the "Great Empire" had 134 departments, from Hamburg to Rome and Barcelona, as well as the Illyrian Provinces, and a population of 70 million (of which only 30 million were from France in 1793), and several vassal states (the Kingdom of Italy), the Kingdom of Naples, the Kingdom of Spain, the Confederation of the Rhine with the Duchy of Warsaw, the Swiss Confederation, the Principality of Lucca and Piombino, the Principality of Erfurt, the Free City of Danzig and finally Corfu, island of the Republic of the Seven Islands still under French control). The Empire was then at the height of its territorial extension, although its overseas colonies fell under British control.

"You must not fight too often with one enemy, or you will teach him all your art of war." - Napoleon Bonaparte

Campaigns from Russia and Germany

Alexander I, pushed by the Russian nobility acquired from the British, refused to cooperate with Napoleon to deliver the final blow to the United Kingdom. Napoleon, believing war inevitable, invaded Russia in 1812. The Grande Armée, swollen with Italian, German and Austrian contingents, became gigantic: 600,000 men crossed the Niemen. The Russians, led by Kutuzov, apply the "scorched earth" strategy, retreating incessantly in front of the French troops. The battle of the Moskova on 12 September was indecisive. Although the Russians abandoned the terrain, losses were almost equal on both sides.

The day after the French troops entered Moscow, the Russians set fire to the city. Napoleon, hoping for a step on the part of Alexander, lingers in Moscow. When he gave the signal to retreat, winter was dangerously close. The Grande Armée begins a desperate race towards Germany through the devastated regions it has travelled through on the way. The cold, snow and Cossacks cause appalling losses. Of the 600,000 men who entered the campaign, only a few tens of thousands crossed the Berezina. The Great Army is destroyed.

Encouraged by this dramatic failure, the kings took up arms again against France.

Despite two victories in Germany (Bautzen and Lutzen), some of his German allies betrayed Napoleon on the very battlefield of the Battle of Leipzig, also known as the "Battle of the Nations", which saw 180,000 Frenchmen and 300,000 allies (Russians, Austrians, Prussians, Swedes) fighting each other. The defeat suffered that day was decisive. Marshal Poniatowski, a Polish prince and nephew of Stanislas II, the last king of Poland, lost his life trying to cross the Elster with his men. There are 100,000 dead and wounded.

French Campaign and first abdication

In 1814 an alliance was formed between the United Kingdom of Great Britain and Ireland, the Russian Empire, the Kingdom of Prussia and the Empire of Austria. Despite a series of victories (battles of Champaubert, Montmirail, etc.) won by Napoleon at the head of an army of young inexperienced recruits (the "Marie-Louise"), Paris fell on March 31 and the marshals forced the Emperor to abdicate. Napoleon's intention was to do so in favor of his son (Napoleon II), but the allied powers demanded an unconditional abdication, which he signed on April 6, 1814.

Napoleon, who thought that the allies were going to separate him from the Empress Marie-Louise of Austria and her son, the King of Rome, took a dose of "Condorcet's poison" during the night of April 12 to 13, which was to enable him to commit suicide. For a long time it was thought to be opium in a little water, Dr. Hillemand thinking that it was an accidental absorption of too much opium intended to soothe abdominal pain, but it seems that this is not the case.

The troubles and the nature of Napoleon's malaise do not correspond to opium intoxication. If he chooses this way of dying, it is because he thinks that his body will later be exposed to the French: he wants his guard to recognize the calm face it has always known him in the midst of battles. In any case, he calls Armand de Caulaincourt to dictate his last wishes.

In full discomfort, the Emperor complained about the slow effect of the substance he had swallowed. He declares to Caulaincourt: "How difficult it is to die, how unhappy it is to have a constitution that postpones the end of a life that I am so anxious to see end! "Napoleon's nausea became more and more violent and he began to vomit. When Doctor Alexandre-Urbain Yvan came, Napoleon asked him for an extra dose of poison but the doctor refused, saying that he was not a murderer and that he would never do anything against his conscience. The doctor himself has a nervous breakdown, runs away on horseback, and no one sees him again.

The agony of the Emperor continues, Caulaincourt leaves the room to ask the valet and the interior service to keep silent. Napoleon calls Caulaincourt back, telling him that he would rather die than sign the treaty. The effects of the poison dissipate and the Emperor can resume his normal activities.

He was subsequently deposed by the Senate on April 3 and exiled to the island of Elba, according to the Treaty of Fontainebleau signed on April 11, retaining the title of Emperor but reigning only on this small island. His convoy from Fontainebleau to the Mediterranean Sea before embarking for Elba Island passed through royalist Provencal villages that booed him. He risked being lynched in Orgon, forcing him to disguise himself.

Napoleon's farewell speech to the Old Guard

On April 20, 1814 before being exiled to Elba Napoleon dedicated a short speech to the soldiers of the Old Guard.

The following is the speech:

"Soldiers of my Old Guard: I bid you farewell. For twenty years I have constantly accompanied you on the road to honor and glory. In these latter times, as in the days of our prosperity, you have invariably been models of courage and fidelity. With men such as you our cause could not be lost; but the war would have been interminable; it would have been civil war, and that would have entailed deeper misfortunes on France.

I have sacrificed all of my interests to those of the country. I go, but you, my friends, will continue to serve France. Her happiness was my only thought. It will still be the object of my wishes. Do not regret my fate; if I have consented to survive, it is to serve your glory. I intend to write the history of the great achievements we have performed together. Adieu, my friends. Would I could press you all to my heart."

Fact: It is said that Napoleon carried a vial of poison, attached to a cord he wore around his neck, that could be swiftly downed should he ever be captured. Apparently, he did eventually imbibe the poison in 1814, following his exile to Elba, but its potency was by then diminished and only succeeded in making him violently ill.

The Hundred Days

In France, Louis XVIII dismissed "Napoleon II" and took power. Napoleon is worried about the fate of his wife and especially his son who is in the hands of the Austrians. The royalist government soon refuses to pay him the promised pension and rumors circulate about his deportation to a small island in the South Atlantic Ocean. Napoleon therefore decided to return to the continent to regain power.

The Napoleon route and the "Flight of the Eagle".

- March 1, 1815: Disembarking at Golfe-Juan, Napoleon and his small troop reach Cannes, where they arrive late and leave early.

- March 2: Wanting to avoid the Rhone route, which he knew to be hostile, Napoleon then took the road to Grasse to reach the Durance valley via the Alps. Beyond Grasse, the column takes bad mule tracks and stops at Saint-Vallier, Escragnolles, and Séranon.

- March 3: After a night's rest, the troop reaches Castellane; in the afternoon it reaches Barrême.

- March 4: Napoleon finds the road in Digne and stops in the evening at the Malijai castle, impatiently awaiting news from Sisteron, whose citadel, commanding the narrow passage of the Durance, may block his way.

- March 5: Sisteron is unguarded and Napoleon lunches there, then leaves the locality in an atmosphere of budding sympathy. In the evening, he arrives in Gap and receives an enthusiastic welcome.

- March 6: he sleeps with Corps.

- March 7: He reaches La Mure, then finds in front of him, in Laffrey, troops sent from Grenoble. It is here that the famous episode that is commemorated today by a monument in the "prairie de la Rencontre" (Meadow of Encounter) is located. That same evening, Napoleon made his entrance into Grenoble to the cries of "Vive l'Empereur" (Long live the Emperor).

The armies sent to stop him welcomed him as a hero everywhere on the road that today bears his name. Marshal Ney, who had sworn to Louis XVIII to bring Bonaparte back to him in an iron cage, bowed down before his former sovereign, which would make him the only marshal executed for treason during the Second Restoration. Napoleon arrived in Paris *without a blow.* This ascent to Paris is known as the "Flight of the Eagle", inspired by Napoleon's words: "The Eagle will fly from bell tower to bell tower to the towers of Notre-Dame".

In 1932, the Napoleon road was inaugurated between Golfe-Juan and Grenoble. Flying eagles mark out this course.

Return to power and final defeat

The flight of Louis XVIII and Napoleon's return to the Tuileries on March 20, 1815 marked the beginning of the period known as the *Hundred Days*. Napoleon had the *Acte additionnel aux Constitutions de l'Empire* (*Additional Act to the Constitutions of the Empire)* drawn up (drafted on 22 April 1815, approved on [1] June). A House of Representatives was elected.

Battle of Waterloo

"You become strong by defying defeat and by turning loss and failure into success." - Napoleon Bonaparte

On the international level, Napoleon affirmed his peaceful will, but the allies did not accept this return and took up arms again against France. The great European powers such as England, Prussia and Austria, whose representatives had met in Vienna, decided to relaunch the war against the Emperor, whom they considered "Outlawed by the Nations". The Allies sent massive numbers of troops to Belgium.

On 18 June 1815 the Battle of Waterloo took place south of Brussels, where Napoleon was preparing to face the coalition. Napoleon had to defeat the Prussian armies of Blücher and the English armies of Wellington. Napoleon gave Grouchy the mission to take care of the Prussians, and Ney to take care of the English. The two commanders will have difficulty in agreeing on their strategy, and will make a series of mistakes. The junction of the Prussian and British armies, which could not be prevented by Marshal Grouchy, overcame the imperial troops. Ney, slow and bad in his choices, will make the cavalry lose. Napoleon felt that the outcome of the battle was defeat. After ten hours of battle, the French retreat. The French army organizes its retreat by the road to Charleroi. This defeat forced Napoleon I to abdicate for the second time on June 22nd 1815.

He returned to the Élysée Palace on June 21, 1815. On the 22nd, he abdicated, declaring in writing: "I offer myself as a sacrifice to the hatred of the enemies of France," and "I proclaim my son, under the name of Napoleon II, Emperor of the French. As the armies of the Seventh Coalition drew closer to Paris, he left the palace on the 25th for the Château de Malmaison, then on the 29th he took the road incognito in an isolated carriage (dressed as a bourgeois) to Rochefort, then Fouras, where two frigates, *La Saale* and *La Méduse, were* waiting for him, wishing to join the United States.

On July 8, he embarked for the island of Aix and boarded *La Saale*. François Ponée, commander of *La Méduse*, offered the emperor to fight the HMS *Bellerophon*, while *La Saale* commanded by Pierre Philibert would pass. But Philibert refused to play this role which was reserved for him. Joseph Fouché, president of the provisional government, alerted the British to the risk of Napoleon's flight. Several English corvettes escorting the *Bellerophon* were sent to the Antioch sluice, forcing Napoleon to negotiate.

Seeking asylum from the "most constant of his enemies", England, he was first taken in charge by the *Bellerophon*, then transferred on August 7, 1815 to *Northumberland*, which deposited him on the island of St. Helena, in the middle of the Atlantic Ocean. He was not given the opportunity to set foot in England, as the British ministers were determined to prevent Napoleon from seeking asylum by invoking *Habeas corpus*.

The return of Napoleon and his final defeat made France's international situation even more precarious. The Allies treated it more harshly in 1815 than during the Treaties of Vienna. Indeed, Napoleon left France bloodless.

Demographically, it has lost approximately 1,700,000 men since 1792, the majority of them during the Napoleonic Wars. It is economically ruined. Its ports and arsenals are also ruined. The country has lost all its remaining colonies from the Ancien Régime. Its international influence, established since Richelieu and Louis XIV, is reduced to nothing. The national territory is reduced to a smaller extent than under Louis XVI. The Saarland and the towns of Marienbourg, Philippeville and Landau, acquired under Louis XIV, were ceded to the coalition.

Moreover, this territory is occupied, and the country has to pay a heavy war indemnity for the maintenance of the foreign troops established on its soil.

Last years

Exile in St. Helena

Napoleon was deported and imprisoned by the British on St. Helena Island, first commanded by Admiral Cockburn and then by Sir Hudson Lowe. The Emperor was accompanied by a small troop of loyalists, including the Grand Marshal of Bertrand Palace, the Count of Las Cases, General Montholon, and General Gourgaud. He devotes himself to writing his memoirs, which he dictates to Las Cases. He also tried to learn English; he received several visitors passing through St. Helena, which was then an important stopover for any ship sailing around Africa.

Once installed in Longwood, he avoids going out because Lowe gave the order that the emperor must be under guard everywhere.

On this rock, Napoleon will make friends with a young English girl of about fifteen years old, Betsy Balcombe.

She was one of the Emperor's last friends before he returned to England in 1818. She will take a lock of his hair with her.

Napoleon gradually became ill and weakened. By January 1819, his condition was critical, but was more or less well diagnosed and treated by the doctors on the island. In the second half of April 1821, he wrote himself his last will and several codicils, about forty pages in total.

Death

Napoleon died at the age of 51, on May 5, 1821, "at 17 hours and 49 minutes", making "the most powerful breath of life that had ever stirred human clay" (Chateaubriand). His last words are: "France, army, Josephine", or, according to the *memoirs of St. Helena*: "head... army... My God! "Nerval, in his poem À *la mort de l'Exilé,* notes: "The last words of Napoleon's dying were: 'My God and the French nation... French... my son... armed head...'. We do not know what these words meant. ", and a current version claims that he actually said: " tête d'armée ", which is much less enigmatic.

Hudson Lowe, English governor of St. Helena Island and jailer of Napoleon, declared before his deathbed :
The cause of his death was immediately the subject of controversy: English doctors officially concluded that he died of stomach cancer, but François Antommarchi, a Corsican doctor who arrived on the scene in 1819, refused to agree with these conclusions after his detailed autopsy - which had been ordered in advance by the Emperor - which showed, among other things, a very degraded

spleen, liver and gall bladder, a stomach full of ulcers and a perforated ulcer miraculously blocked by the liver.

Napoleon's death would thus result from the combination of an ancient chronic hepatitis, a stress related stomach ulcer evolving to perforation, a degeneration of this ulcer into carcinoma and, immediate cause, the aggravation of the whole by an aberrant medication (antimony and mercury), the coup de grâce having been delivered by the English doctor Arnott, who inflicts on the patient an extravagant dose of 10 grains of calomel while the normal dose is one or two grains, which causes a severe stomach hemorrhage that will be fatal. A lively discussion then opposes the various doctors and officials, resulting in a kind of political compromise presenting "cancerous squirre with pylorus" as the cause of death, which allows Napoleon's death to be attributed to a family predisposition, therefore to a most natural death, since his father and sister Elisa died of the same disease.

Because of the differences of opinion that appear in the later accounts of some, the cause of Napoleon's death has been the subject of various theories. One hypothesis frequently put forward is that Napoleon was deliberately poisoned with arsenic trioxide. This theory, first put forward by the Swedish stomatologist Sten Forshufvud, is rejected by a large number of historians. The medieval historian Michel Pastoureau, for example, suggests that arsenic was present in the wallpaper and green drapes that the Emperor liked and used at Longwood.

However, following new analyses, Dr. Pascal Kintz, President of the International Association of Forensic Toxicologists, wrote in his article *Three series of analyses of Napoleon's hair confirm chronic exposure to arsenic* (24/01/2008) that "Taking into account these scientific data, we can conclude that Napoleon was indeed the victim of chronic arsenic mineral poisoning, and therefore rat poison". These conclusions are also shared by the International Museum of Surgical Sciences and the International College of Surgeons of Chicago.

His death in 1821 did not put an end to his legend. Indeed, historians have shown the existence of a rumor, which persisted until the beginning of the Third Republic, that the Emperor did not die. As a sign of the rural world's attachment to the myth of a Napoleon Saviour, incessant rumours have been circulating in the French countryside since the end of the Restoration until 1870, lending credence to the rumour that the Emperor, still alive, was about to return to power to preserve the egalitarian gains of the French Revolution.

"Death is nothing, but to live defeated and inglorious is to die daily." - Napoleon Bonaparte

Health status

If Napoleon's death highlighted the health problems he suffered during his exile in St. Helena, his whole life was marked by pathological disorders of varying degrees of severity.

During his autopsy his height was measured at 5 feet, 2 inches, 4 lines, which corresponds to 1.69 m. With a sturdy and enduring constitution, he could ride for several hours without feeling tired. General Bonaparte appeared in his lean and slender youth, and in the years to come he became almost obese at the time of his exile.

In 1785, he suffered from a fever while he was in Auxonne as a lieutenant. From 1786 on, he was afflicted with malaria and suffered from fever in intermittent attacks until 1796. In 1793, he contracted scabies during the siege of Toulon, of which he kept after-effects throughout his life, forcing him to take baths to soothe itching. Talleyrand and the actress Mademoiselle George witnessed seizures which were assimilated to epilepsy.

He mainly suffers from abdominal problems, including chronic pain on the right side, and liver problems, as well as dysuria, the aggravation of which was noted during the Russian campaign. Napoleon did not wear his hand in his vest to relieve stomach pain. This gesture encountered in official portraits, was a posture inspired by the oratory attitude of the philosopher Eschine, and is found in other 18th century portraits. It was thus a posture regularly adopted by officers in their official portraits to avoid having their arms dangling, as recommended in *The Rules of Decorum and Christian Civility,* a book written in 1702 by John Baptist de La Salle.

Return of his ashes to France

Napoleon asked to be buried on the banks of the Seine, but when he died in 1821 he was buried in St. Helena.

Nineteen years after Napoleon's death, King Louis-Philippe I was able to obtain the return of Napoleon's ashes from the United Kingdom.

The exhumation of the body took place on October 15, 1840 and Napoleon left the island of St. Helena for good on Sunday, October 18, 1840. His body was triumphantly repatriated to Paris on December 15, 1840, in the midst of an innumerable crowd, and buried at the Invalides, in "a large sarcophagus [...] of red porphyry - in fact, adventurous quartzite from Finland, close to porphyry - placed on a base of green granite from the Vosges". The black marble base comes from the marble quarry of Sainte-Luce. The transport of this block, 5.5 meters long, 1.20 meters wide and 0.65 meters thick, was not without difficulty.

After 1854, Emperor Napoleon III negotiated with the British government the purchase of Longwood House and the Valley of the Tomb (St. Helena), which became French property in 1858 and has since been managed by the Ministry of Foreign Affairs.

Napoleonic Heritage

Few figures have left such an important trace as Napoleon Bonaparte in French historiography and political thought. This imprint seems to be due in large part to the *Memorial of St. Helena,* an essay published by Las Cases in 1823 two years after the emperor's death, which met with great editorial success. For Jean Tulard, the *Memorial* became the breviary of Bonapartism. In 2014, some 80,000 titles have been dedicated to the Emperor, laudatory works with a few exceptions, even if it is currently approached with more critical distance.

In the middle of 1799, the state of France was catastrophic. The French government was shaken by internal problems, taxes were not reaching the state coffers, banditry had grown, roads were being broken down, recently conquered regions and satellite states of the French Republic were threatened by the general offensive of the Second Coalition armies in Switzerland, Italy, Southern Germany and Holland, Trade was at its worst, industry (especially silk in Lyon) was ruined, unemployment was on the rise, the price of bread was too high for the workers, hospitals were not working... This was the moment that Bonaparte, who was still a revolutionary general at the time, chose to abandon his army in Egypt and go up to Paris, fomenting a coup d'état, on November 10, 1799.

Surrounded by a halo of prestige (he has just emerged victorious from the Italian campaign and the Egyptian campaign is, for the time being, still a success), he finds little resistance and public opinion does not disavow him. But the republicans are worried: does Napoleon embody the definitive advent of the values of the Revolution, or does he promise, on the contrary, the destruction of revolutionary thought? We can consider today that Napoleon will solidify the legacy of the Revolution in more than one way; if he ends the Republic and stops the revolutionary movement, he will remain faithful to the principles of the Revolution, which he will seek to export on a European or even world scale. The Consulate, in short, objectifies this movement.

The Consul Napoleon Bonaparte, thanks to a series of measures, allows the Revolution to take place over time. Bonaparte will first work to create new institutions, which will endure until today.

The new constitution he had drafted strengthened the executive branch at the expense of the legislature and created a centralized administration, organized into specialized and standardized directorates and ministries (including the new Ministry of the Interior, entrusted to Fouché). He kept the administrative divisions created during the Revolution. These strong institutions strengthened the authority of the state, revived the country and removed the risk of a return to the Ancien Régime. The state coffers are bailed out. Napoleon also decided to pacify certain conflict zones by developing an innovative urban policy. Thus, Pontivy was enlarged and the city of La Roche-sur-Yon was created in 1804. The prefecture of the Vendée remains the only city entirely created by Napoleon.

Then, Napoleon Bonaparte is in the line of the Revolution. After the coup d'état, the institutions changed, but the majority of those who would hold positions were already in place at the time of the Directoire: in the assemblies created by the Constitution of An X, most senators, tribunals or members of the Conseil d'État had already held positions of responsibility under the previous regime; prefects were chosen from the revolutionary assemblies. This allowed Bonaparte to better control the opposition. The reforms he introduced were the logical continuation of those already undertaken during the Revolution. The financial and commercial reforms attributed to him were, for part of them, imagined by the members of the Directoire.

They had already attempted the continental blockade that Napoleon would implement against the United Kingdom in 1806. Even some of the war techniques used by Napoleon and of which he is considered the inventor had already been implemented during the Revolution. The drafting of a French Civil Code itself had already been undertaken during the Revolution.

In addition, it stabilizes the political landscape by pacifying the country and thus guarantees the long-lasting existence of its government. The peace signed with the Vendée royalists in December 1799 marked a great step forward in the appeasement of the country, which no government had previously managed to achieve.

The signing of the Concordat in 1801 enabled Napoleon to secure the support of many Catholics who had been hesitant until then, and the royalists lost as many, one of the fundamental reasons for the population's support for this movement being the anti-Catholic nature of the Revolution. This Concordat, which did not establish Catholicism as the dominant religion and which could have been seen as a desire to return to the Ancien Régime, allowed Bonaparte to obtain a new legitimacy and to establish his authority a little more. The Concordat maintained the sale of national assets. Thanks to these two treaties, Bonaparte neutralized the royalist opposition and seemed to be part of the revolutionary legacy.

Finally, the French Civil Code is a revolutionary work. Begun in 1800 and finally published in 1804, it replaces all previous law, and retains meritocracy, egalitarian taxation, conscription, freedom of enterprise and competition as well as labor, enshrines the disappearance of the feudal aristocracy, and in principle equality before the law. By preserving and enshrining in the Code all these achievements of the Revolution, Bonaparte allowed them to pass through the regimes and reassured a large part of the population.

But Napoleon also suppressed many revolutionary achievements. First of all, revolutionary cults were abolished. The freedoms of expression, assembly, movement and the press were suppressed in favor of an authoritarian state and increased surveillance of the population, orchestrated by Fouché. The equality proclaimed in the Civil Code was not respected: Women depended on their husbands; the bosses had great power over the workers, as the workers' passbook reduced them to quasi-serfs; slavery was re-established in the colonies; Then, the establishment of the prefects, who are the equivalent of the stewards, the creation of the Council of State, the equivalent of the king's council, of a new nobility based on notability, the false plebiscites organized (votes are invented, there is no secret vote, one ratifies a fait accompli...) make the Jacobins fear the worst. The spectre of a return to the monarchy haunts them.

Finally, by becoming in turn First Consul, Consul for life and then Emperor, he finished with the Republic. The public favor allows him to write the Constitution of the year VIII, which gives him the reality of the powers and especially does not mention the national sovereignty. This constitution divides the legislative power, which from that moment on will lose all influence. It was during the year X that the transformation of the still republican regime into a despotism that only lacked a crown took place. The post of First Consul for life sounded the death knell for the Republic.

Above all, these regime changes allowed Napoleon to be less and less dependent on his successes or failures and gave him another dimension vis-à-vis other European leaders. Napoleon thus also suppressed a good number of revolutionary achievements.

Napoleon stops the revolutionary movement but not the Revolution. By gaining the confidence of the bourgeoisie (thanks to the sale of national goods, maritime and continental peace, the creation of a meritocratic nobility...), thanks to the prestige of great victories (Marengo, 1800), to the successful resolution of crises such as that of 1802 (famine and unemployment), Napoleon gained popular support and gradually freed himself from the revolutionary process, which was no longer necessary. Over the years, as his popularity continued to grow, he would rise in power and distance himself from the Republic.

In 1804, after various plots aimed at his assassination and the resumption of hostilities with the United Kingdom, he was perceived as the only bulwark against the enemies of the Revolution, and the question of heredity became a matter of concern. He takes advantage of this to be crowned Emperor (or rather, to be crowned himself). What could be seen as the culmination of a tyrant's project is not. Indeed, at the time of the coronation, Napoleon declared himself to be in the continuity of the Revolution, and was supported by the revolutionaries themselves, despite the end of the revolutionary process.

The imperial wars perpetuated the Revolution. In all the conquered countries, Napoleon I imposed the Civil Code and consequently all the revolutionary notions that were part of it. He is considered at first as the liberator of Europe.

But from the Fourth Coalition, which began in 1806, the aim of these wars would no longer be the propagation of revolutionary ideas. In spite of the Napoleonic defeat of 1815, the ideas of freedom and equality would remain firmly established in the countries that had been conquered, and many upheavals would follow in the course of the 19th century.

Thanks to the modernization of French and European institutions, the pacification of the country, his military victories and the conquest of most of Europe, Napoleon allowed the expansion and perpetuation of the Revolution.

Thus, despite the many regime changes during the 19th century, the French Civil Code will remain in force throughout Europe, and the many revolutionary principles it contains. Napoleon was thus more the continuator than the assassin of the revolution, despite the impasse he reached over the Republic. By suppressing cults and other revolutionary achievements that endangered the work of the revolution itself, he allowed others to pass through the ages.

"Courage isn't having the strength to go on - it is going on when you don't have strength." - Napoleon Bonaparte

Restoration of slavery

The first abolition of slavery in the colonies on February 4, 1794 and its economic and political consequences led the First Consul to take up the question. As soon as they took office, the three Consuls assured the former slaves that the freedom granted to them by the Convention would be respected.

This was the case until 1802, with the signing of the Peace of Amiens on March 25, 1802, when the United Kingdom had to return the occupied colonies to France. Among these are Saint Lucia and Martinique, which did not benefit from the application of the law of abolition of slavery. In front of this imbroglio between colonies with and colonies without slavery, the consular power decides the *status quo*: the colonies where there is no more slavery will remain free, on the other hand those until then occupied by England will keep the laws previous to the abolition, that is to say the Black Code. A commission made up of Cambaceres and the three State Councillors Dupuy, Régnaud de St-Jean d'Angély and Bruix works on a project which went in the direction desired by Bonaparte. But it appears difficult to make two opposite principles cohabit in the same bill. It was then decided to mention only the case of the territories recovered on the occasion of the Treaty of Amiens, and to mention nothing for the colonies where slavery had already been abolished.

In the maintenance of slavery in Martinique, the First Consul is pushed in particular by his ministers (such as Decrès and Talleyrand) and the Intendant General to the colonies Guillemin de Vaivre, originally from Saint-Domingue, but also by his wife Joséphine, a Martinican woman whose family and several friends had many interests in Martinique. "Slavery as well as the slave trade and the importation of Blacks into the colonies restituted by the treaty of Amiens will take place in accordance with the laws and regulations prior to 1789".

At the beginning of June, he had Toussaint Louverture arrested and deported. Toussaint Louverture had distinguished himself during the slave revolt of Saint-Domingue eleven years earlier and, convinced by the abolition of slavery in 1794, had kept the colony in France. The Antilleans were to die of cold one year later at the fort de Joux, in the Doubs, a department renowned for the harshness of its winters. With the expedition of Saint-Domingue, a second phase of the war of Saint-Domingue begins, it provokes many massacres on both sides. It was the Blacks and Mulattos of Santo Domingo who emerged victorious from these terrible battles and created, in January 1804, the first independent Black Republic of Haiti.

At the end of 1801 in Guadeloupe, Captain General Lacrosse worried in particular the black population which had been free until then.

Finally, the Black troops revolted, ousting Lacrosse and then opposing the army commanded by General Richepance, who had come to restore Lacrosse. These events ended in May 1802 with the resistance of Louis Delgrès, which was strongly repressed and ended with the collective suicide of the insurgents in Matouba. Lacrosse and his successor Ernouf gradually reintroduced slavery in the form of forced labor, and then slavery itself by means of a rural police order of 22 April 1803, which referred to certain articles of the Black Code, and finally with the adoption of the decree of the First Consul, dated July 16, 1802, which states that "The Colony of

Guadeloupe and Dependencies will be governed, like Martinique, St. Lucia, Tabago, and the Eastern Colonies, by the same laws in force there in 1789.

From 1802 to 1803, Guadeloupe went from a regime that recognized the presence of black and mulatto generals and officers in the French army to a regime that granted citizenship only to whites.

During the Hundred Days in 1815, Napoleon decreed the abolition of the "Treaty of the Blacks," in order to please British public opinion, which was largely influenced by the abolitionist movement. His return from the island of Elba mobilized all the European states against him, and Napoleon tried to disrupt the coalition by accepting resolutions taken by the European powers during the Congress of Vienna. His decision was confirmed by the Treaty of Paris on November 20, 1815. Nevertheless, during the Restoration, this abolition was ignored and only reconsidered under British pressure from 1817 to 1831.

Achievements of Napoleon Bonaparte

Under the Consulate

The Consulate is essentially a period of pacification and stabilization of France, after the revolutionary decade. Many institutions are founded, which will then survive long after their creator; they take up some of the achievements of the Revolution and still exist at the beginning of the 21st century in France.

Thus, on December 13, 1799 (22 Frimaire, An VIII), the Constitution of An VIII, drafted by Daunou on the basis of the principles enunciated by Sieyès and Bonaparte, created the Council of State in Article 52. This body was initially responsible for drafting laws to relieve the ministries and was to advise the government on the legislation to be undertaken. In this Constitution, Napoleon Bonaparte also creates the Senate, inspired by the Roman Senate. It is responsible for ensuring that the Constitution is respected and its members are appointed by the First Consul and then by the Emperor.

In 1800, the First Consul Bonaparte created two important institutions that still exist today: on February 13 (24 Pluviôse, An VIII), he established the Bank of France; on February 17 (Law of 28 Pluviôse, An VIII), Bonaparte created the prefectures, headed by a corps of prefects appointed by the First Consul and then by the Emperor and representing the State. All these institutions made it possible to reorganize the administration in France, which had not functioned since the beginning of the Revolution in 1789. This reorganization made it possible to restore order and revive the economy. But internal order was completely restored on July 15, 1801, when Napoleon Bonaparte signed the Concordat with Pope Pius VII reconciling France with the Church, while maintaining the freedom of worship established by the Declaration of the Rights of Man and of the Citizen of 1789. Bonaparte wished to reorganize French society in many areas:

- Education: he launched a major reform that led on May 1, 1802 (11 Floréal year X) to the creation of high schools and the Saint-Cyr Military School.

- Economy: On December 24, 1802, he established the twenty-two chambers of commerce and instituted a new currency, the germinal franc on April 7, 1803 (17 germinal year XI).

- Justice and Law : Bonaparte metamorphoses the French judicial system, he establishes the courts of appeal and the Tribunal de cassation becomes the Cour de cassation. He reorganized law studies with the creation of law schools and a diploma accessible to all, the capacity in law on March 13, 1804 (22 ventôse year XIII). Finally, on March 21, 1804 (30 ventôse year XII), Napoleon Bonaparte promulgates the French Civil Code which defines new rights and obligations for the French. By the law of 19 May 1802, Napoleon Bonaparte also established the Legion of Honour, awarded to military and civilian persons whom the State wished to reward with this distinction for services rendered.

Under the Empire

- In 1806, Emperor Napoleon I ordered the triumphal arch of the Star.

    o On March 18 (21 Germinal Year IX), the first industrial tribunal was created in Lyon.

    o On May 10, the University was recreated, after its abolition by the Revolution, in a form that led to the current universities.

- In 1807, Napoleon entrusted Alexandre-Theodore Brongniart with the construction of the future Paris Stock Exchange.

    o On February 9, he resurrects the function of Grand Sanhedrin (which facilitates the assimilation of Jews in the Empire). Napoleon continued the work of tolerance towards the Jews initiated by the Revolution.

    o On 16 September, Napoleon created the Court of Auditors.

- 1808

    o On March 17, Napoleon creates by decree the baccalaureate.

- 1810 :
    - On February 12, the Penal Code is promulgated.

Legislative work

From the very beginning of the Consulate, Bonaparte has implemented numerous reforms in education, justice, finance and the administrative system. His set of civil laws, drafted by Portalis, Maleville, Bigot de Préameneu and Tronchet and known as the 1804 Napoleonic Code, still has a strong influence in many countries today. It is quite largely influenced by the drafts of the Civil Code presented by Cambaceres during the Revolution, when he was not yet second consul.

Bonaparte presided over many of the sessions for the elaboration of the Civil Code. He considered it with pride as his major work: "My glory is not to have won forty battles [...] What nothing will erase, what will live forever, is my Civil Code, it is the minutes of the Council of State. ».

The French Civil Code is, however, very largely inspired by a range of diverse laws and customs already existing under the Ancien Régime which it unified. Its administrative work continued until 1814. Among other reforms, it began the work of cadastral surveying of French territory.

This Civil Code was widely exported, which was a major phenomenon in universal legal history.

In architecture and urban planning

In Paris

Napoleon had many monuments erected in Paris, several of which were dedicated to the glory of the Grande Armée and its victories.

He had two triumphal arches built after the victory at the battle of Austerlitz after having declared to his soldiers: "You will only return to your homes under triumphal arches". The first to be ordered is the triumphal arch of the Star in 1806 to make it the starting point of a triumphal avenue crossing the Louvre and Place de la Bastille, it will be completed only in 1836. The second is the triumphal arch of the Carrousel, built from 1806 to 1808 and located on the Place du Carrousel, west of the Louvre. The Battle of Austerlitz is also commemorated by the Vendôme

Column, formerly called the *Austerlitz Column and* then the *Column of the Grande Armée,* built between 1805 and 1810. It is surmounted by a statue of Napoleon.

The church of the Madeleine was also to be a temple to the glory of the Great Army, as planned in 1805. In 1812, after the Russian campaign, Napoleon changed his mind and returned to the project of a church. It was finished in 1842. Napoleon also built from 1807 to 1825 the Brongniart Palace in Corinthian style to house the Paris Stock Exchange. He also had the Palais d'Orsay built from 1808 to 1840 to house the Conseil d'État.

Napoleon had the capital developed. He had the streets of Rivoli, Castiglione and the Pyramids pierced and the buildings in Paris numbered. He ordered the connection between the Louvre and the Tuileries Palace and the completion of the square courtyard of the Louvre (construction of the west and south wings) which became a museum. He gave the Palais Bourbon a new facade, erected between 1806 and 1810. He had three bridges built (the Pont des Arts (1801-1803), the Pont d'Austerlitz (1802-1806) and the Pont d'Iéna (1808-1814)) and several dozen fountains such as the elephant of the Bastille. He embellished the Luxembourg Garden and created the Jardin des Plantes, the Ourcq, Saint-Martin and Saint-Denis canal. Finally, He had the Père-Lachaise cemetery laid out.

Outside the Paris Region

- The foundation of Napoleon (the current city of La Roche-sur-Yon).

- The transformation of Place Bellecour in Lyon.
- The column of the Grande Armée near Boulogne-sur-Mer.
- The stone bridge in Bordeaux.
- The construction of Piazza della Pace (Milan) in Milan.
- The construction of Fort Napoleon in La Seyne-sur-Mer.
- The canal from Nantes to Brest and Mons-Condé.

"If you wish to be a success in the world, promise everything, deliver nothing." - Napoleon Bonaparte

Titles and honours

Title

- August 15, 1769 - October 16, 1795: Mr. Napoleon Bonaparte

- October 16, 1795 - November 10, 1799 : Mr. General Napoleon Bonaparte

- November 10, 1799 - May 18, 1804 : Mr. General Napoleon Bonaparte, First Consul of the French Republic

- May 18, 1804 - April 6, 1814: His Imperial Majesty the French Emperor

    - March 17, 1805 - April 11, 1814: His Majesty the King of Italy

    - July 12, 1806 - October 19, 1813: His Imperial Majesty the Emperor of the French, Protector of the Rhine confederation

- April 14, 1814 - February 26, 1815 : His Serene Highness the Sovereign Prince of Elba Island (*exile*)

- March 20, 1815 - June 22, 1815: His Majesty the Emperor of the French (Hundred Days)

Foreign Decorations

- From 1805 to 1811, Napoleon I received more than fourteen foreign decorations. The following is a complete list of all the orders of which the emperor was decorated by date of award:

    o 1805: Knight of the **Order of St. Hubert** (Bavaria)

    o 1805: Knight of the **Order of the Black Eagle** (Prussia)

    o 1805: cordon of the orders of **Christ**, **Aviz** and **Santiago** (Portugal)

    o 1805: Knight of the **Order of the Golden Fleece** (Spain)

    o 1805: Knight of the **Order of the Golden Eagle** (Württemberg)

    o 1806: Grand Cross of the **Order of Fidelity** (Baden)

    o 1807: Grand Cross of the **Order of St. Joseph** (Würzburg)

    o 1807: Knight of the **Order of Saint Andrew** (Russia)

    o 1807: Knight of the **Order of the Street Crown** (Saxony)

- 1807: Grand Cross of the **Order of Merit** (Hesse)
- 1808: Knight of the **Elephant Order** (Denmark)
- 1809: Dignitary of the **Order of the Two Sicilies** (Naples)
- 1810: Knight of the **Order of the Seraphim** (Sweden)
- 1810: Grand Cross of the **Order of St. Stephen** (Hungary)
- 1810 : Grand Cross of the **Order of Leopold** (Austria)

Contemporary Perspectives

Jean-Antoine Chaptal writes: "Napoleon used newspapers himself to wage war on his enemies, especially the English. He personally wrote all the notes that were inserted in *Le Moniteur,* in response to diatribes or assertions that were published in the English gazettes. When he published a note, he believed he had convinced. It will be remembered that most of the notes were neither models of decency nor examples of good literature; but nowhere did he imprint better the stamp of his character and his kind of talent. »

Nicknames

- *Nabulio* : nickname given as a child by his mother Letizia Ramolino ;

- *La Paille-au-nez*: nickname given by Napoleon's comrades to the school of Brienne. Indeed, with his Corsican accent, Napoleon pronounced his first name *Napoillioné* ;

- *General Vendémiaire* : nickname given by other generals of the Republic as a sign of contempt for this fact of arms of internal repression of royalist civilians, after Bonaparte's intervention during the royalist insurrection of 13 Vendémiaire year IV;

- *The Little Corporal*: nickname given by the soldiers on the evening of the Battle of Lodi Bridge in 1796. The rank of corporal used as a nickname was given to him according to a military custom of affection to salute a brave behavior ;

- *Boney*: nickname given by British cartoonists, diminutive of "Bonaparte". In reference to the English word "*bone*", it can thus be translated as "*the bony*". This nickname referred to General Bonaparte's meagre figure in the early years of his military career up to the Consulate. This nickname played on the contrast with the plump John Bull, symbol of the English and his opulence in the face of a France perceived as ruined and hungry during the Revolution;

- *Le Petit Tondu* : nickname given by soldiers from the Consulate and the beginning of the Empire after Bonaparte had his hair cut (on his return from the Egyptian expedition in 1799) and enforced a new regulation for military haircuts (abandoning long hair and wigs in favor of the "Titus cut");

- *Buonaparte* : reuse of the Corsican name spelled in this way in the first years of Napoleon Bonaparte's life, by his French royalist adversaries and by the British who did not recognize his imperial dignity acquired after the rupture of the peace of Amiens (1803) and thus refused to use only his first name, sign of his title;

- *The Usurper*: nickname coming from royalist circles, from the establishment of the Empire and Napoleon Bonaparte's claim to monopolize sovereign power. The term is mainly used when the Bourbon reestablishment is realistic, then effective, in 1814 and then in 1815 during the Hundred Days;

- *The Tyrant*, *the Ogre*: nicknames commonly given by his opponents and caricaturists, especially at the end of the Empire when the military effort of conscription weighed more and more heavily on the population;

- *Le Père-la-Violette* : the *violet* is the flower of hidden love. After his first abdication, it was believed that he would return to the time when violets blossomed, and this was realized; the violet became a rallying sign for the Bonapartists after the Second Restoration ;

- *John of the Sword*: nickname given by the soldiers of the Grande Armée, particularly within the Imperial Guard at the time of the return from the island of Elba ;

- *Nicolas*: nickname used particularly by the royalists of the South of France, where the Devil is sometimes called so. Caricatures of the time thus designate Napoleon by this other first name, with the effect reinforced by the same initial letter "N";

- *Lou Castagnié* ("The Chestnut Tree"), nickname given in the South of France and which refers to Napoleon's Corsican origins, chestnuts being a famous specialty.

Privacy Policy

Historical influences

During his youth, Bonaparte showed admiration for certain statesmen, notably Pasquale Paoli, a Corsican independence fighter, and Mirabeau, a moderate revolutionary. He also greatly admired Rousseau, even saying: "Oh! Rousseau! Why do you have to have lived only sixty years! In the interest of truth, you should have been immortal! "He later denied these ideas, as Rousseau's ideas proved to be inconsistent with the consular and then imperial system. During the Revolution, he hoped to be able to overcome his modest living conditions thanks to the new regime put in place and was therefore favorable to this evolution. He even wrote on a banner stretched over his native house: "Long live the Nation! Long live Paoli! Long live Mirabeau! »

He is also grateful to the Robespierre brothers, Augustin and Maximilien, to whom he owes his rapid rise in rank. He later sent a pension to their sister. He wrote to Tilly: "I was a little affected by the catastrophe of Robespierre whom I loved and believed to be pure, but even if he was my brother, I would have stabbed him myself if he aspired to tyranny".

Napoleon had great admiration for the military genius of Turenne. In 1800, he had his tomb transferred to the dome of the Invalides.

Bonaparte shows more than one admiration for great conquerors and emperors. He is depicted wearing a laurel wreath and a toga to show himself as Julius Caesar and Augustus for example. He is also fascinated by Frederick II.

Napoleon and Women

Although married twice, Napoleon cultivated throughout his life several mistresses (fifty-one according to some historians) who gave him illegitimate children. This descent is important to him, confirming his belief that he was not sterile. Two mistresses will play a great role in his life.

Napoleon's first great mistress was Éléonore Denuelle, lady of the palace and reader of his imperial majesty Josephine: she gave him his first child on December 13, 1806, who was named Léon.

The second, he met her during the Polish campaign. On January ^{1}, 1807, the Emperor enters Warsaw, a young woman makes her way to him, it is Marie Laczynska, Countess Waleswka, twenty-six years old, wife of an old man, Anastase Walewski. During a ball given in honor of the Emperor, the Poles wish that Marie Walewska be in his bed: they thus form the wish that the fate of Poland, divided between Russia, Prussia and Austria, could change with the help of Napoleon. At first very reluctant, she ends up being in love with the Emperor and gives him a son, Alexander, born on May 4, 1810.

As for his wives, he has two: one he is very much in love with, Josephine de Beauharnais, and another, Marie-Louise of Austria, who is only a political wife, charged with giving him an heir to the imperial throne. According to Josephine, Napoleon only loved two women: herself and Countess Walewska.

Napoleon and spirituality

Napoleon and Catholicism

Napoleon was born into a Catholic family and was baptized on July 21, 1771.

His position towards Catholicism sometimes seems more a matter of political calculation than of personal choice, but he declares that he has a real attachment to his native religion:

"It is certain that, in the disorder which I succeeded to, that on the ruins where I found myself, I could choose between Catholicism and Protestantism; and it is true to say again that the dispositions of the moment were all in favor of the latter; but, besides the fact that I really cared about my native religion, I had the highest motives for deciding. By proclaiming Protestantism, what did I obtain? I would have created in France two great, almost equal parties, when I wanted them all to disappear; I would have brought back the fury of the quarrels of religion, when the lights of the century and my will were to make them disappear altogether. These two parties, by tearing each other apart, would have annihilated France, and would have made her the slave of Europe, when I had the ambition to make her the mistress of it. With Catholicism I was much more sure to achieve all my great results: in the interior, at home, the great number absorbed the small, and I promised myself that I would treat the latter with such equality that there would soon be no more reason to know the difference. On the outside, Catholicism kept me the pope: and with my influence and our forces in Italy, I did not despair sooner or later, by one means or another, of ending up having the leadership of this pope to myself; and then what an influence! What a lever of opinion on the rest of the world! »

At the end of his life, Napoleon received the extreme unction from the hands of Father Vignali. Moreover, article 1 of his will, written on April 15, 1821 in St. Helena, is very clear on this subject: "I die in the apostolic and Roman religion, in whose bosom I was born more than fifty years ago.

Napoleon and Islam during the Egyptian Campaign

Napoleon's interest in Islam seems to be dictated by the context. The Egyptian campaign was prepared in the same way as the Italian campaign, that is, in the hope of rallying the local population to the French cause. In the aim of this rallying, everything is done so that Egyptians, who are mostly Muslims, feel valued. Napoleon declared to his soldiers on board the ship *l'Orient* on June 22, 1798 that: "The people we are going to live with are Mohammedans [...]. Do not contradict them; act with them as we did with the Jews, with the Italians; have regard for their muftis and imams, as you did for the rabbis and bishops.

This strategy is clearly visible in proclamations aimed at the population, such as the one of July 2, 1798 in Alexandria: "People of Egypt, you will be told that I have come to destroy your religion; do not believe it! Answer that I have come to restore your rights, to punish the usurpers and that I respect more than the Mamelucks, God his Prophet and the Alcoran".

For General Dupuy, who accompanied Napoleon during the Egyptian campaign, this interest in Islam was simulated for political reasons: "We deceive the Egyptians by our simulated attachment to their religion, in which Bonaparte and we do not believe any more than in that of Pius the deceased".

On July 17, 1799, he addressed the notables of the province of Aboukir and pronounced what is akin to a declaration of faith in Islam: "There are no other gods but God and Muhammad is his prophet". However, if the act of conversion to Islam is final when the *Shahada* is pronounced, the believer must demonstrate sincerity and determination. This *Shahada* pronounced by Napoleon is however a ruse intended to "reduce the number of his enemies". No other source allows us to affirm that he converted to Islam.

Napoleon's Personal View of Islam

Napoleon was fascinated above all by the Orient. Regarding the prospect of converting to Islam, he states that "after all, it is not impossible that circumstances would have led me to embrace Islamism. ...] But it would only have been in the right direction; I would have had to go at least as far as the Euphrates. The change of religion can perhaps be understood by the immensity of its political results. In a more general way, Napoleon does not seem to want to convert when he expresses himself on the Concordat: "I really cared about my native religion.

Napoleon emphasizes the proximity of the Christian and Muslim religions when he depicts the prophet:

"Mohammed [...] who walks so closely in the footsteps of Christianity, and departs from it so little" and notes the differences existing on St. Helena: "Analyzing in the most ingenious way the two religions of the East and West, he said that ours was all spiritual, and Mohammed's was all sensual; that punishments dominated in our country: It was hell and its eternal torments, while it was only rewards for the Muslims: the beautiful-eyed *houris, the* laughing hedgerows, the rivers of milk; and from there he concluded, by opposing the two religions, that one could say that one was a threat, it presented itself as the religion of fear; that the other, on the contrary, was a promise, and became the religion of attractions.

Napoleon's ambivalence towards Islam was due to the need for double language during the Egyptian campaign: on the one hand, speeches admiring Islam or favorable to its interests held by religious authorities, and on the other hand, personal confessions which often only came into play much later and gave a point of view that the years made distant.

For Henry Laurens, if Napoleon's interest in Islam was inspired by political concerns, he was nevertheless "truly fascinated by Islam and the East [and] his admiration for Islam is essentially for the creator of societies, the Prophet Mohammed.

"Religion is, in fact, the dominion of the soul; it is the hope, the anchor of safety, the deliverance from evil. What a service has Christianity rendered to humanity!" - Napoleon Bonaparte

Napoleon and Freemasonry

Among the military and intellectual entourage close to Napoleon many are Freemasons (General Kleber who founded the lodge "Isis" in Cairo, Dominique Vivant Denon, member of the Sacred Order of Sophisians and the lodge "The Perfect Reunion", Gaspard Monge member of the military lodge "The Perfect Union"). Also a rumor claims that Bonaparte may have been initiated into freemasonry during the Egyptian campaign in the lodge "Isis", as suggested by the manuscript *The Mirror of Truth* dedicated to all masons, the fact that he was a wolf cub (i.e. the son of the freemason Charles Bonaparte) and that he did not contest the fact that he was later called "brother" by various members of the 1,200 Masonic lodges that developed during the First Empire, nevertheless the criticisms of the freemasons he held during his exile on St. Helena seem to prove the contrary.

Correspondence

Napoleon Bonaparte maintained an abundance of correspondence, partly for private use, but above all an important official correspondence. During his lifetime, some of these letters were published, either individually or in collections, but often with the aim of exaltation or, on the contrary, polemic. For example his 75 notes and letters to Count Lazare Carnot, his Minister of the Interior during the one hundred days published in Brussels in 1819.

In the 1850s, Emperor Napoleon III had his uncle's correspondence published. If this new publication also has a propaganda purpose, it will be more serious than what had been done until then.

However, some letters were not found, others were deliberately omitted, and the text was sometimes redacted under various pretexts. When the last volume of Napoleon I's correspondence appeared in 1869, the officer Louis Rossel demonstrated that the books of strategy attributed to him by the commission in charge of publishing the correspondence were not and cannot be his. In the following years, new letters were published, often in the form of specific collections (letters from Napoleon to the same correspondent). Others reappeared punctually.

Since 2002, the Fondation Napoléon has been engaged in a vast undertaking of scientific publication of all the Emperor's correspondence. To this end, it has launched an appeal to retrieve documents that might be found in various archives or libraries, and especially from private individuals.
For edition references, see below.

Family

Ancestry

Parents

- Charles Bonaparte

- Maria Letizia Ramolino

Brothers and Sisters

The list below gives the names of the 26 legitimate children of Napoleon's brothers and sisters, in order of birth. Other children, those who died at a very young age or from relationships outside of marriage, are not listed.

Nephews and nieces

Two nephews died during Napoleon's lifetime (Dermid Leclerc and Napoleon Charles Bonaparte, the latter having been considered heir presumptive to the imperial crown between 1804 and 1807 according to the constitution), and two were born after his death.

Uncle

- Joseph Fesch, Cardinal, Bishop of Lyon and Primate of the Gauls. He is in fact the uterine brother of Napoleon's mother, Maria Letizia Ramolino. Her mother, Angèle-Marie Pietra-Santa, widow of Jean-Jérôme Ramolino, married François Fesch, a Swiss officer in the service of the Republic of Genoa.

Marriages and children

Napoleon married twice:

- a first time on March 9, 1796 with Josephine de Beauharnais, who was later crowned empress; this marriage remaining childless, it ended in a divorce, pronounced by a senatus-consulte on December 16, 1809;

- a second time, on April 2, 1810 with Archduchess Marie-Louise of Austria, who gave him a son eleven months later: Napoleon François Joseph Charles Bonaparte (March 20, 1811-22 July 1832), King of Rome, Duke of Reichstadt, also known as Napoleon II, although he only reigned in theory for fifteen days between Napoleon's second abdication and the Second Restoration.

Napoleon was engaged on April 21, 1795 to Désirée Clary (1777-1860), sister of Julie Clary, herself married in 1794 to Joseph Bonaparte. But Napoleon met Joséphine de Beauharnais in Paris on October 15, 1795, through his friend Paul Barras, and made him renounce the plan to marry Désirée, not without a guilty conscience as evidenced by his correspondence with Désirée.

Napoleon also had at least two natural children, both of whom had descendants:

- Charles, Count Léon (1806-1881), son of Éléonore Denuelle de La Plaigne (1787-1868).

- Alexander, Count Walewski (1810-1868), son of Countess Walewska (1789-1817).

And according to more or less contested sources :

- Napoleon Louis Charles Bonaparte (1802-1807), eldest son of Louis Bonaparte.

- Jules Barthélemy-Saint-Hilaire (1805-1895) whose mother remains unknown.

- Emilie Louise Marie Françoise Joséphine Pellapra (1806-1871), daughter of Françoise-Marie Leroy, married Louis Marie Joseph de Brigode, and posterity ;

- Eugen Alexander Megerle von Mühlfeld (de)(1810-1868), son of the Austrian Victoria Kraus (de).

- Auguste Alfred le Pelletier de Bouhélier (1816-1868), employee, from where two children :

    - Edmond (1846-1913), journalist, deputy of the Seine, deputy mayor of Bougival, whose posterity: the writer Saint-Georges de Bouhélier and Isabelle, who became the wife of René Viviani.
    - Laure (born in 1852), who married Alphonse Humbert (1844-1922), deputy of the Seine, and posterity.

- Josephine de Montholon, daughter of Countess Albine de Montholon (born in St. Helena on January 26, 1818, died in Brussels on September 30, 1819).

Order of succession to the imperial throne in July 1815

With Napoleon II, there were 25 Napoleonides of the second generation, including 17 living in the Hundred Days. After the fall of the Empire, in this generation, there were four male heirs, in order of succession :

1. Napoleon II (who had already briefly inherited the imperial throne in 1815) ;

2. Napoleon-Louis Bonaparte ;

3. Louis-Napoleon Bonaparte (Napoleon III) ;

4. Jerome Napoleon Charles Bonaparte.

For the order of succession of subsequent contenders to the imperial throne, see : Bonapartist pretenders to the imperial throne of France.

Preservation of the personal archives of Bonaparte and his family

- The personal papers of the Bonaparte family, including the correspondence of Napoleon I, are kept in the National Archives under the symbol 400AP (Fonds Napoléon) and 176AP (Fonds Bonaparte).

"History is a set of lies agreed upon." - Napoleon Bonaparte

Enjoy all our books for free…

  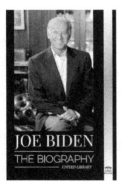

Interesting biographies, engaging introductions, and more.

Join the exclusive United Library reviewers club!
You will get a new book delivered in your inbox every Friday.
Join us today, go to: https://campsite.bio/unitedlibrary

BOOKS BY UNITED LIBRARY
Kamala Harris: The biography
Barack Obama: The biography
Joe Biden: The biography
Adolf Hitler: The biography
Albert Einstein: The biography
Aristotle: The biography
Donald Trump: The biography
Marcus Aurelius: The biography
Napoleon Bonaparte: The biography
Nikola Tesla: The biography
Pope Benedict: The biography
Pope Francis: The biography
Bitcoin: An introduction to the world's leading cryptocurrency
And more…
See all our published books here:
https://campsite.bio/unitedlibrary

ABOUT UNITED LIBRARY
United Library is a small group of enthusiastic writers. Our goal is always to publish books that make a difference, and we are most concerned with whether a book will still be alive in the future. United Library is an independent company, founded in 2010, and now publishing around up to 50 books a year.

Joseph Bryan - FOUNDER/MANAGING EDITOR

Amy Patel - ARCHIVIST AND PUBLISHING ASSISTANT

Mary Kim - OPERATIONS MANAGER

Mary Brown - EDITOR AND TRANSLATOR

Terry Owen - EDITOR